Love Unlove

Saeema Madhiya Abrahani

/ BookLeaf
Publishing
India | USA | UK

Made with ❤ on the BookLeaf Publishing Platform
www.bookleafpub.in
www.bookleafpub.com

Dedication

To all the girls who are waiting for the Hero to save the day, look in the mirror.

Preface

This book was my outlet.
My escape.
They say a heartbreak rewrites your character,
but they don't tell you that it also builds it.
If you are holding this book, know that each word here is
not just mine but yours too.
As cliché as it sounds, no love is greater than self love.
May that love find you, empower you, make you
unbreakable, invincible.
Just remember, you're worth it.
You've always been worth it.

Acknowledgements

*To all the boys who promised me the moon and the stars
and everything in between and terribly failed to deliver,
Thank you.
To the heartbreak that cracked open my inner poet,
Thank you.
Most importantly to the one who loved every damaged
piece of me like it was art.
I love you.*

1. A Mystical Night

In a room full of hundred and one,
He found her and was completely undone.
His heart soared screaming as though it had just won.
He did not blink for an eternity fearing that
she would run.
His eyes followed her through the night,
Every bone in his body singing that
She was his Ms. Right.
And when they finally met under the moonlight,
He couldn't utter a word,
his lips were sealed so tight.
Until he realised it was impolite,
he shook her hand to greet her and his entire being was
suddenly alight.
And that's when he knew for sure, that his life without
her, would never be just right.

2. She

*The promise of beauty was molded into every line and
feature of her face.*
*She was destined to be more exotic than fragile,
more wilderness and less serene.*
*She had eyes that sparkled more with laughter
and less modesty.*
She was more stubborn and less docile.
She was light, love and power.
She was the amber pit of nostalgia.
She was more petals than thorns.
She was more chaos than calm.
She was vintage.
She was fire.
She was grace.
She was magic and a little bit of poetry too.
She was the rebellion and the cause.
*She was everything that was and everything that was yet
to be.*
She was You.

3. Kinds of Love

They say there are three kinds of loves in your life.
The first where you're naive.
The Epic where you sacrifice.
And,
The True which demands nothing, but your time.
But her first love was everything all at once.
It was the kind you never fall out from.
It was the kind that both destroys and heals you.
It's always the kind that you never wake up in the arms of forever.
It was the only one that taught her to measure her forever in moments and not years.
Her first love was everything all at once.
For that's when she learnt that,
loving with all she has is still not being in love enough.

4. Amateur Lover

The beauty is in being an amateur lover.
The idea isn't to have a perfect candlelit dinner.
The beauty is to walk in the pouring rain.
To cuddle on a cozy winter night.
To find the rights in the wrongs.
To make them smile while their eyes shine with unshed tears.
The idea is not to find the Romeo to my Juliet.
The idea is never to grow old together.
The beauty is in finding someone you can forever be a child with.

5. Home

Maybe he was the one that got all of you.
Maybe he was the one that made you reckless and out of control.
Maybe he was the one that gave you sleepless nights filled with magic.
Maybe he was the one that got under your skin and made you unsteady.
Maybe he was the one who said all the right things and did them too.
Maybe he was the one who crosses your mind when you are under a starlit sky.
Maybe he was the one that you remember on a cozy night.
Maybe he was the one who made you believe in all the love songs.
Maybe he was the one who made you feel like a Christmas wish.
Maybe he was your first, your last and your ever.
Maybe he was the one.
The one your heart called Home.

6. Over Again

I am not a complicated girl,
I just want someone to write sonnets for me.
I want the boombox over your head kind of love.
I want you to slow dance with me while we bake cookies
at midnight.
Kiss me on top of the ferris wheel.
Watch fireworks with me in Disneyland.
I am not a complicated girl,
I just want to fall in love for the first time over and over
again.

7. Love me

You expect the love you think you deserve.
Well, if you ask me.
I think I deserve the moon and the stars and everything
in between.
But do you think, I deserve that ?
Magical nights dancing under the moonlit sky.
Confessions of love under the arbor filled with my
favorite flowers.
Emeralds that match the color of my eyes.
I say, love me.
Love me only if you think I deserve to be loved on days
when you think its the hardest to love me.

8. The Sign

She was always looking for signs.
It was the way he looked at her, and then he didn't.
It was the way her laughter made him laugh,
and then it didn't.
It was the way he held her close enough to never let go,
and then he didn't.
It was the way he wanted to make her feel special, and
then he didn't.
It was the way he loved, he cared, he longed, he desired,
and then he didn't.
It was then she realized,
That maybe looking for signs was the sign.

10. I Dare You

Unlove the way my lips feel pressed against yours,
Unlove the way I fit perfectly in your arms,
Unlove the times you watched me fall asleep,
Unlove the mornings you woke up to me feeling
complete,
Unlove the way my smile makes you crazy,
Unlove the way my eyes make you feel dreamy,
Unlove the way my heart touches your soul,
Unlove me,
I dare you.

10. Void

In the middle of a perfectly happy day,
I feel it,
I feel it creeping upto me,
I feel its claws marking my soul,
I feel the uneasiness,
I feel the gaping hole in my chest again.
I have this desperate urge to fill it,
To fill this void.
Sometimes with meaningless conversations with
strangers,
Sometimes with the world between my favorite pages,
Sometimes with the music on soo damn loud that it can
dull the ache.
In the middle of a perfectly happy day,
Sometimes I feel like my world is falling apart.

11. Poison

I chose my own poison,
I knew it all along,
That's why I was guarded,
That's why I wouldn't give it all,
Oh! But I have cried a river,
And burnt all the bridges down,
But darling, now I am unreachable.
I chose my own poison,
And I knew it all along,
That chaos doesn't harm,
It's my calmness that's worst than my storm.

12. She woke up

She woke up at the crack of dawn,
Feeling anxious and desolate,
Her life played on repeat in her mind,
And that's when she realized,
She always loved the wrong ones,
She always loved too many,
They ripped her heart open,
And left her bleeding.
Sometimes he was too much of a man,
Sometimes he was too less of one.
She woke up at the crack of dawn,
And that's when she realized,
It wasn't a heart they all lacked,
It was merely a spine.

14. She listens

She listens,
She listens to your sorrows and your misery,
She listens to the guilt that's eating you up alive.
She listens to you go and on about how unsatisfied you
are with your perfectly privileged life,
She listens when you mistake the glimmer of her hollow
eyes into a sparkle of mischief.
She listens when all you do is try to break her spirit,
Try to simmer her down,
Try to crush her soul,
Try to break her heart time and again.
All she does is listen,
She listens to all of you,
While all you ever want is to silence her down.

15. A Part of Me

A part of me will always hold onto you,
A part of me will always skip a beat,
A part of me will always dance with you in the dim lights of your room,
A part of me will always feel the warmth of your endless hugs,
A part of me will always feel the cold wind blowing as we ride into the sunrise,
A part of me will always want to run away with you in the mesmerizing sunsets,
A part of me will always be yours,
A part of you will always be a part of me.

16. You said Forever

You said forever,
You said forever and I gave you my heart
right from the start,
You said forever and then you went ahead and
crushed all of me,
You said forever and now I am stuck with your memories
playing in my mind and I can't sleep,
So I am not going to give up on you and me.
You said forever so now I keep breaking my own heart
on repeat,
And I have left a million pieces of it on your street,
You said forever,
But now I know it was just an illusion of you and me.

17. Universe

It's the Universe,
It keeps putting me in your path,
It's the reason for those faint dreams you can't remember
about me,
It makes you wish you remembered how it felt to thread
your fingers with mine and
hold it close to your heart,
So I could hear how insanely it beats around me,
It makes you want to reach out to me even when you
know I am not yours.
It's the Universe,
It makes you fall in love with me even when we are
centuries apart.

18. Dreams

It's the dreams that are the worst,
Everything I ever want to say to you plays behind those
shutters,
Everything I want you to do to me leaves me feeling
disoriented and talking in stutters,
I wake up with a hollow feeling,
I wake up wanting you like I used to,
Only now it isn't right to want you to hold me tight.
It's the dreams that are the worst,
For they are the missing puzzle pieces that I wish were
never sought out.

19. Bad Boy

His eyes are crazed,
His actions deranged,
He will leave you feeling absurd and insane,
Oh Baby,
He is not the bad boy you should crave,
He is nothing but harebrained.
He is a storm that will cause havoc and leave everything
unhinged in its wake.

20. Worth

What's worth dying for, if not love? They said.
Well I say, why should I die for love?
Why can't I live for it?
Why should I compromise for it?
Why can't it accept me the way I am?
Why should I let it go?
Why can't it embrace me?
Why should I set it free?
Why can't I fight for it?
What's love dying for, if not love? They said.
Well I say, if it wipes you off the slate it wasn't love to
begin with.

21. A Story I'll never write.

Yours and mine,
It's a story I will never write,
I don't know how to put into words the moments that
became memories,
Memories that sometimes hit me soo hard in the middle
of a perfectly happy day, that I just stop.
I don't know where I am anymore and I feel empty,
I feel soo empty inside and suddenly I don't know why I
am breaking and hurting.
It's like my heart is bleeding, but not all at once.
I just want it to hit me hard and be done,
But the pain, it lurks in the shadows,
It comes out only when I am about to forget you again.
That's why yours and mine is a story I will never write,
Because I could never find the words to describe you and
me.

22. The Secret

The secret is to stop pretending,
It's okay to be broken,
It's okay to fall apart,
It's okay to love the monsters,
It's okay to scream in the storm,
It's okay to make empty promises,
It's okay to break them all,
It's okay for your heart to be dark,
It's okay to want to destroy it all.
The secret is to stop pretending.
Because Its okay.
It's okay to be human.

23. Let go

She never missed the red flags,
She saw not one but too many,
But It was the love,
The illusion of it was deceiving,
Or maybe she just wanted to see a similar face in a
crowded room,
Maybe she just wanted to know It was okay to not be
okay and that she could fall apart and he would still be
there to not let her break apart.
But It was 4am,
And she was hurting soo bad,
And her heart was exhausted,
And she finally realized she had to let go,
Because no matter how insanely she loved him,
She wasn't in love with him anymore.

24. Prince Charming

She is her own prince charming,
She isn't a damsel in distress,
She is enchanting and alluring,
But sometimes she is also a complete mess,
You don't have to scale a tower to save her,
You definitely don't have to kiss her awake,
So don't try to dumb her down,
Don't try to steal her crown,
Don't try to toss her opinions through the drain,
Because she is her own prince charming,
Oh Baby!
She is most definitely her own Soul Mate.

25. Love Letters

There is something insanely romantic about hand
written love letters,
Imagine someone sitting under the moon lit sky pouring
their love for you into a million words,
Imagine the stars witnessing their shinning eyes and
their ink stained souls,
Imagine the sigh that leaves their lips when they realize
they just want to hold you close,
There is something insanely romantic about hand
written love letters,
Imagine being loved just like used to in the olden days.

26. Deep

I want us to be deep,
I want us to be like the bottomless mimosas on a Sunday
afternoon,
I want to know why you rewind the entire song to listen
to that one line over and over again,
I want to know what goes on in your mind when we
drive past the ocean and you look out into nothingness,
I want to sleep under the starlit sky with you by my side,
our fingers intertwined,
I want to walk bare feet with you into the crashing
waves by the shore,
I want us to be deep,
Because I don't want to feel empty anymore.

27. Not her

I am not her,
My heart doesn't skip a beat when I see you,
My soul doesn't somersault in your presence,
I don't spend my nights writing about you,
I don't spend my days dreaming about you,
I am most definitely not the woman
who is going to kneel,
I am not her,
And why would I want to be,
When you're lying with her in the dark,
wishing it was me.

28. Patriarchy

Time and again,
We have been told to hold on to things that break us,
They tell you It's all going to be okay at the end,
And all you need to do is compromise,
It's the patriarchy,
They tell you that you are asking for too much,
When in reality It's not about you,
It's about them not being able to get out of their comfort
zone,
It's about them feeling intimidated by your ambitions
and your confidence,
It's not about you baby girl,
It never was,
It's about the tale as old as time,
Where you are made to believe you need him to fight
your battles,
When in reality you are very capable of slaying the
dragons on your own.

29. Fling

You can tell her how much you love her,
You can scream It out for the world,
But that doesn't necessarily mean
you are in love with her,
There is a very fine line between being in love with
someone and loving the idea of being in love with
someone,
Her flaws and temper,
Her insecurities and break downs,
It's all a part of her,
And when you choose to not love those,
Then you aren't loving all of her,
So how can you claim to be soul deep in love with her,
When you can't love her at her weakest.
It's more complicated than you think,
Being in love is a full time thing,
And if you're only looking for the happy hours,
Then darling,
This is just a fling.

30. Stop Romanticizing

You need to stop romanticizing his behaviour,
Ofcourse he has changed,
You obviously don't feel loved anymore.
Have you ever stopped and wondered that it was never
about you?
That it was always about him?
The chase, the flowers, the midnight conversations,
Those long walks when the sky was pouring down,
Was it because he wanted the girl he thought he loved?
Where were you in that relationship?
You seriously need to stop and ponder,
You need to stop!
Stop romanticizing his behaviour,
Ofcourse you don't feel loved anymore,
Because maybe he never was,
And maybe he never will.

31. And Suddenly

And suddenly,
You talk too much,
You don't feel right,
You are soo uptight,
Your smile is too dim,
Your eyes don't glint,
You always fight for your rights,
You are not like her,
You don't sit with your lips shut tight,
And suddenly,
You're not enough,
Not good enough to be by his side.

32. Replayed

He looked into her eyes, and said "I am sorry."
While she replayed,
She replayed,
The nights she cried herself to sleep,
The times he walked out on her,
The days he made her feel like she wasn't enough,
The bitter conversations that were
engraved in her mind,
Those empty promises,
Those hollow apologies,
The moments he told her that she was replaceable,
The infinite times he broke her already broken heart,
Until she finally pressed pause,
And flicked the switch off,
And she said "Its okay."

33. Layers

There were infinite layers to her,
Layers she did not want to peel off,
Layers she thought made her vulnerable,
Layers once peeled she thought would expose her,
Little did she know,
Those were the layers that would make her strong,
That she wasn't getting exposed,
She was merely embracing her scars and battles,
That people won't judge,
That the sheer beauty of being human is that they accept
everything that is damaged,
They convert it into art and inspiration,
The sheer beauty of being human is that they always see
themselves beyond the cracks.

34. Not Until

You can't feel it,
Not even a little bit,
Not until you completely let go,
Not until the walls of resistance come down,
Not until you let him reach deep inside you,
Not until you swallow every last
ounce of conscience away,
Not until you ride the very demon that
makes you afraid,
You can't feel it,
Not even a little bit,
Not until you stop fighting to be awake.

35. Cold Dark Room

Empty handed and forlorn,
She was standing in a cold dark room with her soul
barbed and worn,
Her kind eyes distant and torn,
She was standing in a cold dark room
Clutching her daggered chest all alone,
All the love from her veins bleeding dry,
She was standing in a cold dark room,
Begging herself to never even try.

36. Too Late

Sometimes you try to,
Most of the times you can't,
You get manipulated into thinking
they are in love with you,
It's this perfect facade that the world sees,
And in all the ways it could go,
You would be the only one who would come out looking
like a villain,
But after the haze clears,
You see the love for the manipulation it always was.
But by then it's too late.
And I know people say it's never too late,
But in reality there are times,
Times when it's too late.

37. Nostalgia

Nostalgia,
It doesn't hit you on a lonely night,
It slowly grows on you,
On a beautiful rainy evening when you're sitting with
the one you love,
And you remember how your eyes
met across the room,
And as cliché as it sounds,
Time did stand still.
Yes, the butterflies so fondly talked about were real,
And yes, the stars seemed to shine brighter when he was
around,
But as the rain drops then kissed my face,
And my love looked into my eyes like he saw the world
in them,
That's when I realized that maybe,
I was never the girl he was meant to end up with all
along.

38. Poles apart

We are poles apart you know,
He likes large crowds and a chanting stadium,
I find euphoria between my favorite pages curled up on a
cozy evening,
His love is immeasurable,
And I love in bits and pieces,
He looks into my eyes like he sees the world in them,
I look into his overwhelmed by the love I see in them,
We are poles apart you know,
He loves me enough for the both of us,
And somehow I can never love enough
even for one of us.

39. This world of mine

I was sitting under the starlit sky,
Turning the pages of your life,
Wanting to get lost in your eyes,
That dazzling smile made my knees go weak,
Everytime you were hurt my heart grew bleak.
At the crack of dawn I realized,
You were not by my side,
And when I turned around to find you,
Find you in a world that is not my own,
I knew this world,
This world that my heart whispered was home.

40. Peace

Sometimes I am envious,
Envious of those who feel loved,
Envious of those who can love,
But be still my heart,
For I have heard the heart that knows love,
Knows no peace,
And maybe to give up on love is the cruelest thing,
But be rest assured that there is peace in the coldest of
hearts,
And I want that peace again,
I want to unlove again.

41. Deception

If deception was an art,
He created the masterpiece,
He was an artist so fine,
you wished you had what was mine,
He played his part so well,
you would think he was a saint and I was the wrench,
The grass is full of thorns this side,
tearing at whatever is left of me inside,
If deception was an art,
He created the masterpiece,
He convinced you it was all real, and you were naive
enough to believe.

42. Decade

A decade of drama,
A decade of deceit,
A decade of drowning myself in grief,
A decade of dullness,
A decade of despair,
A decade of doubting myself and that's so unfair.
A decade of desperation,
A decade of depression,
A decade of dissatisfaction you can read in his stare.
A decade of disdain,
A decade of dread,
A decade of damage that is beyond repair,
A decade of disillusion,
A decade of defraud,
A decade,
A decade of damnation and my ultimate downfall.

43. To the love of my life.

I did not fall in love with you,
Definitely not at first sight,
It was the way you looked at me,
It was your eyes,
Those melted pools of chocolate held a promise of a love
soo deep that I was sure It would consume us both.
It was the calmness of my heart around you,
The warmth seeping from yours into mine,
It was when you loved me for all the parts of me that
made sense to you,
And even more for all the parts that didn't.
I did not fall in love with you,
Not at first, not somewhere in between, not yet,
I gloriously walked into love with you.

44. Mosaic of love

Humans, so quick to judge, so reluctant to love.
Humans, who pride themselves in
being independent individuals.
Humans, who live in plausible deniability.
Are we whole on our own? I dont think so.
We are made up of light and love,
Of experiences and adventures,
Of sadness and sorrows, of choices and mistakes.
Who am I? If you ask me.
I am not whole.
I am bits and pieces of my children's laughter.
I am scattered splinters of my mother's heart.
I am my father's generosity,
I am my sister's courage,
I am my best friend's kindness,
I am my husband's love.
Who am I? If you ask me.
I am a Mosaic,
A mosaic of everyone's whose loved me and everyone
who I have ever loved, even for a heartbeat.